The Oxford Book of Tudor Anthems

34 anthems for mixed voices

Compiled by Christopher Morris

MUSIC DEPARTMENT

OXFORD
UNIVERSITY PRESS

OXFORD
UNIVERSITY PRESS

Great Clarendon Street, Oxford OX2 6DP, England
198 Madison Avenue, New York, NY10016, USA

Oxford University Press is a department of the University of Oxford.
It furthers the University's aim of excellence in research, scholarship,
and education by publishing worldwide

Oxford is a registered trade mark of Oxford University Press
in the UK and in certain other countries

ISBN 0-19-353325-1   ISBN 978-0-19-353325-7

The cover illustration is reproduced by permission of the
British Library Board from Additional MS. 35324 f. 37$^\mathrm{v}$.

Processed and printed by
Halstan & Co. Ltd., Amersham, Bucks., England

Preface

by Sir David Willcocks

The word 'Tudor' in the title of this collection of anthems is used loosely to cover about 100 years embracing most of the 16th century and the first quarter of the 17th century, a period sometimes described as the Golden Age of English church music.

The thirty-four anthems, selected from the work of fourteen composers whose lives spanned this period, reflect many styles, ranging from simple four-part chordal anthems to elaborate six-, seven-, or eight-part motets of rich polyphony.

Two of the anthems are Verse Anthems, requiring accompaniment. In *Teach me, O Lord*, one of the earliest examples in English church music of the use of a solo voice, Byrd provides an independent organ part to accompany the solo sections. In *This is the record of John*, one of the finest Verse Anthems in existence, Gibbons writes for viols (which can, if necessary, be replaced by organ). The remainder of the anthems are Full Anthems, which may effectively be sung unaccompanied, though they were probably originally performed with accompaniment.

Neither dynamic markings nor indications of phrasing have been suggested by the Editors, but expressive contrast is clearly required in any performance which is to be fully satisfying. In homophonic passages all the voices should normally grade the tone similarly, consideration being given to the general mood of the text, the natural verbal stresses, the shape of the melodic line, and the harmonic progression (tension being created and relaxed by composers through suspensions and their resolution). In polyphonic music each part should be phrased so that the interplay of the voices can be enjoyed both by performers and by listeners.

The Editors have taken account of the fact that pitch in the 16th century was approximately a minor third higher than it is now, and have transposed the anthems to keys suitable for performance today. Choirmasters should however feel free to perform the anthems in whatever key best suits the available singers.

In order to achieve good balance and clarity of texture, low-lying phrases may have to be sung with greater intensity than those which are more comfortably placed. Occasionally it may be advisable for some voice-parts (e.g. alto and tenor) to be interchanged or reinforced, though this needs to be done with care and discretion, lest the parts lose their character.

continued overleaf

Although note-values have generally been halved, and barlines have been introduced for convenience, no suggestions regarding tempi have been made, since account needs to be taken of the size of the choir, the flexibility of the singers, the acoustic characteristics of the building, and the nature of the accompaniment (if any). In general, performance should not be so fast that notes of short duration cannot be clearly articulated, nor so slow that the singers cannot sustain the tone through the natural phrase-lengths. Special care should be taken to establish a satisfactory relationship between duple and triple rhythms (e.g. *This day Christ was born, Haec dies*, etc.).

Provision has been made for all the main seasons and festivals of the Church's Year as well as for general use.

DAVID WILLCOCKS

Index of Titles

Anthem	Composer/Editor	NO.	PAGE
Alleluia. I heard a voice	Weelkes ed. Bray	1	1
Almighty and everlasting God	Gibbons ed. le Huray and Willcocks	2	15
Ascendit Deus	Philips ed. le Huray	3	22
Ave Maria	Parsons ed. Steinitz	4	32
Ave verum Corpus	Byrd ed. Morehen	5	44
Call to remembrance	Farrant ed. Greening	6	50
Factum est silentium	Dering ed. Greening	7	57
Give almes of thy goods	Tye ed. Greening	8	67
Gloria in excelsis Deo	Weelkes ed. Collins	9	72
Haec dies	Byrd ed. le Huray and Willcocks	10	84
Hide not thou thy face	Farrant ed. Greening	11	94
Hosanna to the Son of David	Gibbons ed. Greening	12	99
Hosanna to the Son of David	Weelkes ed. Morehen	13	113
If ye love me	Tallis ed. le Huray	14	122
I heard a voice	Tomkins ed. Greening	15	126
Justorum animae	Byrd ed. Greening	16	131
Laetentur coeli	Byrd ed. Bray	17	137
Let thy merciful ears	Mudd ed. Collins	18	147
Lord, for thy tender mercy's sake	Farrant/Hilton ed. Greening	19	152
Miserere mei	Byrd ed. Morehen	20	157
O clap your hands	Gibbons ed. Morehen	21	164
O Lord, arise	Weelkes ed. Bray	22	209
O Lord, in thy wrath	Gibbons ed. Morehen	23	231
O Lord, the maker	Mundy ed. le Huray	24	240
O nata lux	Tallis ed. Greening	25	248
O praise the Lord	Batten ed. Greening	26	251
O quam gloriosum	Byrd ed. Bray	27	256
Salvator mundi	Tallis ed. le Huray	28	273
Sing joyfully	Byrd ed. Morehen	29	287
Teach me, O Lord	Byrd ed. Morehen	30	298
This day Christ was born	Byrd ed. Morehen	31	307
This is the record of John	Gibbons ed. le Huray	32	318
When David heard	Tomkins ed. Morehen	33	332
When David heard	Weelkes ed. Greening	34	343
With all our hearts	Tallis ed. le Huray	28	273

Seasonal Index

Use	Anthem	NO.	PAGE
Advent	Laetentur coeli (*Byrd*)	17	137
	This is the record of John (*Gibbons*)	32	318
Christmas	Gloria in excelsis Deo (*Weelkes*)	9	72
	This day Christ was born (*Byrd*)	31	307
Lent	Call to remembrance (*Farrant*)	6	50
	Hide not thou thy face (*Farrant*)	11	94
	Lord, for thy tender mercy's sake (*Farrant/Hilton*)	19	152
	Miserere mei (*Byrd*)	20	157
	O Lord, in thy wrath (*Gibbons*)	23	231
Passiontide	Ave verum Corpus (*Byrd*)	5	44
	Salvator mundi (Latin text) (*Tallis*)	28	273
Palm Sunday	Hosanna to the Son of David (*Gibbons*)	12	99
	Hosanna to the Son of David (*Weelkes*)	13	113
Easter	Gloria in excelsis Deo (*Weelkes*)	9	72
	Haec dies (*Byrd*)	10	84
Ascension	Ascendit Deus (*Philips*)	3	22
	O clap your hands (*Gibbons*)	21	164
Whitsun	If ye love me (*Tallis*)	14	122
Trinity	Alleluia. I heard a voice (*Weelkes*)	1	1
	With all our hearts (English text) (*Tallis*)	28	273
Dedications	O Lord, arise (*Weelkes*)	22	209
Saints' Days	Factum est silentium (*Dering*) Michaelmas	7	57
	Justorum animae (*Byrd*)	16	131
	O nata lux (*Tallis*) Transfiguration	25	248
	O quam gloriosum (*Byrd*) All Saints	27	256
	This is the record of John (*Gibbons*) St. John the Baptist	32	318
Annunciation	Ave Maria (*Parsons*)	4	32
Evening	O Lord, the maker (*Mundy*)	24	240
Communion	Ave verum Corpus (*Byrd*)	5	44
Thanksgiving and Praise	O praise the Lord (*Batten*)	26	251
	Sing joyfully (*Byrd*)	29	287
Remembrance and Funerals	I heard a voice (*Tomkins*)	15	126
	Justorum animae (*Byrd*)	16	131
General	Almighty and everlasting God (*Gibbons*)	2	15
	Give almes of thy goods (*Tye*)	8	67
	Let thy merciful ears (*Mudd*)	18	147
	O Lord, arise (*Weelkes*)	22	209
	O nata lux (*Tallis*)	25	248
	Teach me, O Lord (*Byrd*)	30	298
	When David heard (*Tomkins*)	33	332
	When David heard (*Weelkes*)	34	343

Index of Composers

Composer	Anthem	NO.	PAGE
Batten, Adrian	O praise the Lord	26	251
Byrd, William	Ave verum Corpus	5	44
	Haec dies	10	84
	Justorum animae	16	131
	Laetentur coeli	17	137
	Miserere mei	20	157
	O quam gloriosum	27	256
	Sing joyfully	29	287
	Teach me, O Lord	30	298
	This day Christ was born	31	307
Dering, Richard	Factum est silentium	7	57
Farrant, Richard	Call to remembrance	6	50
	Hide not thou thy face	11	94
Farrant or John Hilton	Lord, for thy tender mercy's sake	19	152
Gibbons, Orlando	Almighty and everlasting God	2	15
	Hosanna to the Son of David	12	99
	O clap your hands	21	164
	O Lord, in thy wrath	23	231
	This is the record of John	32	318
Mudd	Let thy merciful ears	18	147
Mundy, William	O Lord, the maker	24	240
Parsons, Robert	Ave Maria	4	32
Philips, Peter	Ascendit Deus	3	22
Tallis, Thomas	If ye love me	14	122
	O nata lux	25	248
	Salvator mundi (With all our hearts)	28	273
Tomkins, Thomas	I heard a voice	15	126
	When David heard	33	332
Tye, Christopher	Give almes of thy goods	8	67
Weelkes, Thomas	Alleluia. I heard a voice	1	1
	Gloria in excelsis Deo	9	72
	Hosanna to the Son of David	13	113
	O Lord, arise	22	209
	When David heard	34	343

1. ALLELUIA. I HEARD A VOICE

Edited by
ROGER BRAY

THOMAS WEELKES
(c. 1575–1623)

Revelation 19, 1 & 6

Since this edition presents three options for performance, it is important to consult the Editorial Note on page 14.

This anthem is available separately.

*Accidentals placed above notes are to be used for performance of the 'secular' versions only
  (see Editorial Note—method c.).

Alternative Opening

Editorial Note

Sources:

Durham, Cathedral Library MSS A1, C1–3, C7, C11, C14, C16, C17, C19 (c. 1635–75).

London, British Library MSS Add. 29372–6 (1616).

London, British Library MSS Add. 30478 and 30479 (c. 1670) from Durham.

London, Royal College of Music, MS 1051 (early 17th century).

Oxford, Christ Church MSS 56–60 (c. 1620).

San Marino California, H. E. Huntingdon Library, MS HM 461 (c. 1650).

Tenbury, St. Michael's College MS 389 (early 17th century).

York, Minster Library MS M29 (S) (c. 1640).

Method of performance:

Since the work survives in both 'liturgical' and 'secular' sources two clearly different methods of performance seem appropriate; if the correct transposition is applied, a third method may be added:

a. As printed, as a verse anthem, following the Durham reading, observing verse directions. It should be noted, however, that verse allocations are for the transposed version (method b. below), and the choirmaster must mark changes for an untransposed verse performance, as follows (assuming his Bass 1 singers are Decani, and that he has two singers per side): 23, Bass 1 should be 'Verse Dec.2', and Bass 2 should be 'Verse Can.1' / 32 B2 Can.2 / 38 B1 Dec.2 / 42 B2 Can.1 / 45 B1 Dec.1.

b. As above, but transposed up a minor third, for Treble, Mean, Alto, Tenor, Bass. It is no coincidence that Weelkes uses the same music as that found at 'And ever shall be' in the *Nunc dimittis* of his service 'For Trebles'. This is presumably the correct contemporary church performance, and is indicated additionally by the verse allocations, which take into account the fact that all five of the voices are present on both sides of the choir. Thus, for example, the rather odd sight of 'Verse Can.' for Bass 1 (b.23) is not an anomaly because, when transposed, this part is for Tenor. Verse indications are shown in MSS by the simple expedient of omitting whole phrases from the book of the voice which is not to sing them.

c. At printed pitch, unaccompanied, using alternative opening, and performing 'Full' throughout. This very likely represents contemporary chamber performance and is suitable for smaller churches and choirs today.

If method c. is selected, the following accidentals should be altered: (I.17.6.F♮ means that in the highest voice at bar 17 note 6 the F should be natural). I.17.6.F♮ / I.18.2.F♮ / I.56.6.F♮ / I.57.2.F♮ / I.62.6.F♮ / I.63.2.F♮ / II.21.4.F♮ / III.20.1.C♯ / III.59.1.C♯ / V.13.4–5.F♮ / V.52.4–5.F♮. These have been printed above the notes.

I acknowledge the help of Miss Sally Dunkley in the preparation of this edition, though the final solution to the problem of two versions is my own responsibility. A complete critical edition would have involved a lengthy commentary, and one is available in *Musica Britannica* Vol. 23, page 1. Small accidentals and small notes are editorial. Cautionary accidentals are in brackets in the voice parts and small in the organ part.

2. ALMIGHTY AND EVERLASTING GOD

15

Edited by
PETER LE HURAY
and DAVID WILLCOCKS

ORLANDO GIBBONS
(1583–1625)

Collect for the Third Sunday after Epiphany

For Editorial Note see page 21.

This anthem is available separately.

© Oxford University Press 1969

Editorial Note

Sources:

The edition is primarily based upon the version printed by John Barnard in *First Book of Selected Church Musick* (1641). Other sources also consulted include: Royal College of Music MSS 1045 (treble), 1046 (alto), and 1047 (tenor)—manuscript part-books belonging to a set originally owned by John Barnard (*c.* 1625); British Library Add. MS 29289 (alto, *c.* 1625); part-books at Durham Cathedral (*c.* 1640), MSS C2, 4, 5, 6, 7, 9, 10, 11, 15, 16, 17, and 19; St. John's College Oxford, MS 180 (bass, *c.* 1630); and York Minster, MS M 29 (S), (bass, *c.* 1640). The organ part is an exact transcription of Durham Cathedral, MS A1 (*c.* 1635); other organ parts are at Christ Church Oxford (MSS 47 and 1212) and the University of California at Berkeley (MS M2 C 645). The anthem seems to have been especially popular during the latter half of the seventeenth century; parts and scores dating from 1660 onwards are to be found at Gloucester Cathedral, the British Library (MSS 17784, 30478 and 30479), St. Paul's Cathedral, St. Michael's College Tenbury (MS 1023), St. George's Chapel Windsor, and at York Minster (the 'Gostling' part-books).

Editorial Method:

Bar lines, small notes, words in square brackets, and ties marked ⌒ are editorial. Spelling and punctuation have been modernised.

Commentary:

There are surprisingly few variants of any substance in the pre-Restoration sources of the vocal parts. Ambiguities of underlay are, however, present in all; the present edition represents a conflation of the least ambiguous versions. Minor rhythmic variants in the organ part (as for example in bar 14) may serve as a reminder that seventeenth-century attitudes to underlay were surprisingly flexible, and that lacking the composer's own copy of the anthem we are only able to guess, in many cases, at the original word-to-note relationship. Note variants are confined entirely to matters of rhythm, and in each case involve an underlay variant: some of the more substantial of these are listed below:

4.II. 1–2: *m* only (D) / 10.III.3–4: *cqq*, not *c.q* (L) / 11.III.3–12.III.1: tied (L) / 24.III.0–3: *ccqq* (D) / 29.III.1–2: *m* only (D & L) / 29.II.1–2: *cqq* (L) (D = Durham; L = Royal College of Music).

3. ASCENDIT DEUS

Edited by
PETER LE HURAY

PETER PHILIPS
(c. 1565 – c. 1635)

Psalm 47, 5

Source:
Philips, *Cantiones sacrae* (Antwerp, 1612)
Editorial Method:
Bar-lines, small accidentals, cautionary accidentals in round brackets, italicised text, and material in square brackets are editorial. A continuous bracket above the notes indicates a ligature, ⌐▬▬▬¬: a broken bracket above the notes indicates a coloration, ⌐ ¬.

Variants:
29.iii.1: ♯(sic)/39.iii.2-42.iii.1: underlay uncertain, and repeat mark only in next phrase/51: time sig. 3/2: note values have been halved.

This edition has been reprinted from *The Treasury of English Church Music* Volume 2 by permission of Blandford Press Ltd.

This anthem is available separately (from O.U.P.).

English version
God has ascended with jubilation, and the
Lord with the sound of the trumpet. Alleluia. The Lord
has prepared his seat in heaven. Alleluia.

4. AVE MARIA

edited by
NICHOLAS STEINITZ

ROBERT PARSONS
(died 1570)

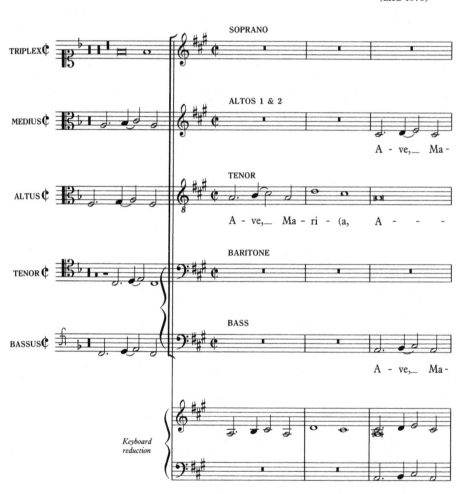

For Editorial Note see page 43.

This anthem is available separately, without keyboard reduction.

¹ Ch. Ch. has C (when transposed equivalent to E).

1) orig. *e'*

English version
Hail, Mary, thou that art highly favoured, the Lord is with thee: blessed
art thou among women and blessed be the fruit of thy womb. Amen.

Editorial Note

The only complete source of this work (apart from Burney's score and other late transcriptions) known to the editor, is a set of part-books at Christ Church, Oxford (MSS. 934-8). The third voice only, however, is also contained in the late 17th century MS., Bodleian Mus. e. 423. Since the fuller underlay given in this version seems to be more accurate than the Christ Church underlay it is added here in round brackets. By analogy some additional underlay has been provided in square brackets in the other parts by the editor.

Note: The opening bars of the third voice seem more appropriate to tenor than alto, and the parts have therefore been distributed S.A.T.Bar.B. in the first eleven bars, and S.A.A.T.B. thereafter, with a slight adjustment in bar 12 to effect the changeover. The three inner parts in bars 11-13 originally ran as follows:-

All small notes are editorial, except for Alto 2, bars 51 and 54, which are from Bodleian. In addition, the following notes, present in sources, have been omitted:

- ⲓⲟⲓ Tenor: Ch. Ch., bar 4, 1st beat
- o Alto 2: Bodleian, bar 35, 2nd beat
- o Alto 2: Ch. Ch., bar 47, 4th beat
- o Alto 1: Ch. Ch., bar 56, 4th beat.

All broken and crossed slurs are editorial. Other slurs are from Ch. Ch. except for Alto 2, bar 55 which is from Bodleian. A slur in Bodleian over all 3 notes in Alto 2, bar 36 has been omitted to avoid confusion if the Christ Church underlay is used. Small accidentals and cautionary accidentals in brackets are editorial.

5. AVE VERUM CORPUS

Edited by
JOHN MOREHEN

WILLIAM BYRD
(1542/3 – 1623)

Source: *Gradualia (I),* 1605. The original text is a Sequence Hymn for Corpus Christi by Pope Innocent VI (*d.* 1342).

Editorial Method: Cautionary accidentals in brackets, and small accidentals are editorial.

This anthem is available separately.

© Oxford University Press 1972

★'unde' in first and second issues (York Minster, 1605, and Christ Church, Oxford, 1610)

* ♩ ♫ 1st time in first issue, both times in second issue (some copies only)

English version
All hail, O true Body, of the blessed Virgin born,
Which in anguish to redeem us did'st suffer upon the cross;
From whose side, when pierced by spear, there came forth both water and blood:
Be to us at our last hour the source of consolation.
O loving, O holy, O Jesu, thou Son of Mary,
O have mercy on me. Amen.

6. CALL TO REMEMBRANCE

Edited by
ANTHONY GREENING

RICHARD FARRANT
(d. 1581)

Psalm 25, 5—6

For Editorial Note see page 55.   This anthem is available separately.

me, O Lord, but ac-cord - ing to thy mer - cy

me, O Lord, but ac - cord - ing to thy _____ mer - cy

me, O Lord, but ac - cord - ing to thy mer - - cy _____

me, O Lord, but ac - cord - ing to thy mer - cy _____

___ think thou on me, O Lord, ___ for thy good - ness.

___ think thou on me, O Lord, ___ for thy good - ness.

___ think thou on me, O Lord, ___ for thy good - ness.

___ think thou on me, O Lord, ___ for thy good - ness.

Editorial Note

Sources:

A	St Michael's College, Tenbury:	MS 1382	[Tenor]	c. 1617
B	British Library, London:	Add. MS 29289	[Alto]	c. 1625
C	Peterhouse, Cambridge:	(1) MS 476	[Alto]	
		(2) MS 478	[Bass]	
		(3) MS 479	[Treble]	c. 1635
		(4) MS 481	[Bass]	
D	Christ Church Library, Oxford:	MS 1001	[Organ]	c. 1640
E	Barnard's *First Book of Selected Church Music*			1641
F	Christ Church Library, Oxford:	(1) MS 1220	[Alto]	
		(2) MS 1221	[Tenor]	
		(3) MS 1222	[Tenor]	c. 1644
		(4) MS 1223	[Tenor]	
		(5) MS 1224	[Bass]	
G	St John's College, Oxford:	MS 315	[Organ]	c. 1660
H	Library of St George's Chapel, Windsor:	(1) MS 1a	[Alto]	
		(2) MS 2	[Alto]	
		(3) MS 2a	[Alto]	c. 1660
		(4) MS 3	[Tenor]	
		(5) MS 4	[Bass]	
I	British Library, London:	(1) Add. MS 30478	[Tenor]	c. 1664
		(2) Add. MS 17784	[Bass]	c. 1675
J	Wimborne Minster Library:	(1) MS P11	[Alto]	
		(2) MS P14	[Tenor]	
		(3) MS P16	[Tenor]	c. 1670
		(4) MS P15	[Bass]	
K	University of California, Berkeley:	MS M2 C645	[Organ]	c. 1670
L	York Minster Library: The 8 'Gostling' part-books			c. 1675
M	Christ Church Library, Oxford:	(1) MS 437	[Organ]	c. 1675
		(2) MS 438		
N	Royal College of Music, London:	Printed Music 1 A 1	[Alto]	c. 1680
O	St Paul's Cathedral, London:	(1) An un-numbered tenor part-book		c. 1680
		(2) An un-numbered bass part-book		
P	St Michael's College, Tenbury:	MS 1023	[Score]	c. 1685
Q	Christ Church Library, Oxford:	MS 440	[Tenor]	c. 1690
R	Bodleian Library, Oxford:	MS Mus. Sch. c 39	[Score]	c. 1695

Other sources which have been consulted, but not collated, for this edition include 3 part-books in the library of Gloucester Cathedral, which were copied from E shortly after the Restoration, the 'Chapel Royal' part-books in the British Library, (Royal Mus. Lib. MSS 23 m 1 –6), dating from the beginning of the 18th century, and J. Bishop's scoring of E made around the middle of the 19th century, and now deposited in the British Library, (Add. MS 30087).

Editorial Method:

Small notes, small accidentals, small rests, and cautionary accidentals in brackets are editorial. The earliest sources have been considered the most authoritative, so variants of textual underlay are not listed. Similarly, discrepancies between the voice-parts and that of the organ have been left as they appear in the MSS sources; so choirmasters must decide in some instances which reading to make use of, (e.g. the false relation in bar 15). This organ part is a conflation of the 5 listed sources *except* in bars 23 and 27 where the earliest part, (D), is quite incompatible with the earliest extant voice-parts – *vide infra*.

Variants:

Bar	/	Stave	/	Beat	/	Source	/	Variant
3–4	/	1	/	3–4	/	P	/	6 beats in upper 8ve in this source
3–4	/	5	/	3–1	/	M(2)	/	G♯ is a tied 1½-beat note
4–5	/	3	/	3–2	/	A	/	upper 4-beat C♯
5–6	/	4	/	1–2	/	J(4)	/	C♯ and F♯ missing
6	/	1	/	3–4	/	C(3)	/	crotchet G♯, followed by crotchet rest
8	/	1	/	2	/	P	/	crotchet C♯ [?]
8	/	5	/	2–3	/	D & M(2)	/	minim F♯
8–9	/	4	/	1–2	/	J(4)	/	2-beat minim slurred for 'O' – 'Lord' is a dotted minim F♯, 'thy' a quaver
10	/	2	/	1	/	J(1)	/	'mercies'
11	/	2	/	3–4	/	C(2)	/	minim C♯ – (Previous underlay not clear)
10	/	4	/	3–4	/	J(4)	/	two crotchets for 'kindness' – rests thereafter
11	/	5	/	1–2	/	M(2)	/	minim E♯ in R.H.
11	/	2 & 5	/	2	/	K & J(9)	/	♯ to alto E ♩ ♩ ♩
13–14	/	1	/	3–2	/	P	/	3 crotchets for 'ev – er of'
12–15	/	1–4	/		/	P & R have 'have' in place of 'hath'		
15	/	4	/	1–2	/	P & J(4)	/	crotchet A♯, crotchet A♮
15	/	4	/	4	/	F(4) & (5), I(2) & L	/	crotchet E
16	/	5	/	3	/	M(2)	/	crotchet B
16	/	2	/	3–4	/	C(1) & J(1)	/	dotted crotchet F♯, quaver E
16	/	3	/	3–4	/	J(1) & (2)	/	dotted crotchet C♯, quaver B
17	/	2–4	/	1–2	/	J	/	dotted crotchet with pause-mark, followed by a double barline
17–18	/	6	/	4–1	/	M(1)	/	bass of L.H. is D♯
17–18	/	6	/	4–2	/	M(2)	/	bass of L.H. is low B
18	/	2	/	3–4	/	B	/	♮ to G
20	/	1	/	1–2	/	E, L, P & R	/	two crotchet Ds
20	/	4	/	1–2	/	P15	/	dotted crotchet, quaver
21	/	4	/	1–2	/	P15	/	four quavers, B, C♯, D and E
21	/	3	/	2–3	/	P	/	lower F♯ for 'of my'
22	/	4	/	1	/	I(2)	/	minim B [?]
22	/	2	/	2	/	J(1)	/	♯ to alto A
23	/	2	/	2	/	C(1)	/	'great' interpolated
25	/	3–4	/	1–2	/	J(2) & (3) & P	/	dotted crotchet, quaver
25	/	3	/	2	/	J(2) & (3)	/	dotted quaver G♯, semiquaver F♯
25	/	1, 2 & 4	/	1	/	C	/	repeat starts, as from 'O remember not'.
27	/	5	/	3	/	M(1)	/	natural to R.H. C [?]
27	/	4	/	3	/	P	/	quavers A and G♯
29	/	1–2	/	1–2	/	J(2) & (3)	/	dotted crotchet, quaver for 'me, O'
29	/	3 & 4	/	1–2	/	P(2), (3) & (4) & P	/	dotted crotchet, quaver
29	/	3	/	2	/	J(2) & (3)	/	dotted quaver G♯, semiquaver F♯
29–30	/	2, 3 & 4	/	3–1	/	J	/	minim with pause-mark, followed by crotchet rest

7. FACTUM EST SILENTIUM

Edited by
ANTHONY GREENING

RICHARD DERING
(d. 1630)

Antiphon to Benedictus at Lauds
on Michaelmas Day

Source: *Cantica Sacra*, Antwerp (1618)

Editorial Method: All small notes in the accompaniment, and in the second tenor in bar 20, are editorial. No attempt has been made to 'correct' the consecutives from the original source. The unfigured bass-line which is provided in the source as the basis for instrumental accompaniment has been amplified to provide support, without attempting a note-for-note *reductio partiturae*.

*See editorial note.

English version
There was silence in heaven whilst the dragon joined battle with
the Archangel Michael. A cry was heard—thousands of thousands
saying: 'Salvation and honour and power be to Almighty God'. Alleluia.

8. GIVE ALMES OF THY GOODS

Edited by
ANTHONY GREENING

Offertory sentence, B.C.P.
from Tobit 4

CHRISTOPHER TYE
(c. 1500-1573)

★The Eb in the source conflicts with the Db in both organ parts, and seems to the editor to be a manifest error
on the part of the scribe.

For Editorial Note see page 71.

This anthem is available separately.

© Oxford University Press 1972

Editorial Note

Sources:

A British Library, Add. Mss 30480–3; four part-books late 16th cent.

B University of California, Berkeley, Ms M2 C645 case B; an organ part early 17th cent.

C Christ Church Library, Oxford, Ms 88; an organ part late 17th cent.

D St Michael's College, Tenbury, Ms 1442; a bass part-book c. 1669.

E Wimborne Minster Library, Mss P11, 14, 15, 17; alto, tenor and two bass part-books c. 1670.

Variants:

Sources D and E both set 'alms' as a single syllable on a minim.

Source	/	bar	/	stave	/	beat	/	variant
E	/	5	/	4	/	4	/	D flat
E	/	6	/	2	/	3-4	/	dotted crotchet A flat, semiquavers G and F for 'thy'
E	/	11	/	2	/	3½	/	semiquavers A flat, B flat
E	/	16	/	2	/	2-3-4	/	minim F, crotchet E natural
E	/	25-26	/	2	/	4-1-2	/	minim F, crotchet E natural
B	/	18	/	5	/	3	/	quavers A flat, B flat in alto
B	/	22	/	6	/	3	/	crotchet E flat in place of rest

Editorial Method:

Small notes in the organ part are editorial.

9. GLORIA IN EXCELSIS DEO

Edited by
WALTER S. COLLINS

THOMAS WEELKES
(c. 1575–1623)

In an earlier edition of this work, by Dr. E. H. Fellowes, the second soprano part was reconstructed by the editor. The missing manuscript has now been found, and the present edition (which contains various other amendments) is a collation of all known early seventeenth-century sources for the anthem, and represents its first appearance in print in the original form. Bar lines have been added, note values reduced by half, and the pitch raised a minor third. The manuscripts used (mostly in microfilm reduction) are: British Library Additional MSS 17,786–91; St. Michael's College, Tenbury Wells, MSS 807–811, and 1382; Christ Church College Music MSS 56–60. The editor wishes to express his gratitude for permission to use these manuscripts to: the British Library Board, the Warden and Fellows of St. Michael's College, and the Governing Body of Christ Church, Oxford.

While performance without instrumental accompaniment would not be wrong, the composer probably would have expected the organ or other instruments to double the voices. The editorial bar lines should not receive regular metrical stress.

Since the publication of this edition in 1960 it has been established that the two soprano parts should probably be reversed, though they are interchangeable for all practical purposes. A complete list of variants is available in *Musica Britannica* Vol. XXIII.

This anthem is available separately.

10. HAEC DIES

Edited by
PETER LE HURAY
and DAVID WILLCOCKS

WILLIAM BYRD
(1543 – 1623)

Source: *Liber Secundus Sacrarum Cantionum* (1591), No. XXXII, William Byrd. British Library, k.2. f.5.

Editorial Method: Bar-lines, the keyboard reduction, and cautionary accidentals in round brackets are editorial. The underlay is carefully indicated in the original, although without the help of slurs. Wherever repeat marks are to be found in the original in place of the full text, the Latin text in this edition has been italicised. From bars 22–41 the note-values have been halved: the time signature in this section is C 3. In the 1591 edition, the word 'alleluia' is printed 'al-le-luy-a', and melismas occur for the most part on 'luy', suggesting that the hard 'i' sound may have been used. The underlay in 20. II. 2 to 22. II. 1 is Dom.cmic.qnusm

This anthem is available separately.

*For these three bars Bass and 2nd Tenor may exchange parts.

English version
This is the day which the Lord hath made:
we will rejoice and be glad in it. Alleluia.

94

11. HIDE NOT THOU THY FACE

Edited by
ANTHONY GREENING

RICHARD FARRANT
(d. 1581)

Psalm 27, v. 10

For Editorial Note see page 97.   This anthem is available separately.

© Oxford University Press 1978

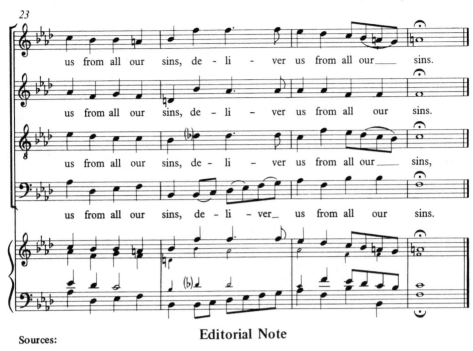

us from all our sins, de - li - ver us from all our_____ sins.

us from all our sins, de - li - ver us from all our sins.

us from all our sins, de - li - ver us from all our_____ sins,

us from all our sins, de - li - ver_ us from all our sins.

Editorial Note

Sources:

A	British Library, London:	Add. MS 29289	[Alto]	c. 1625
B	Shropshire County Records Office, Shrewsbury:	SRO 356 Mus. MS 5	[Bass]	c. 1625
C	Christ Church Library, Oxford:	(1) MS 1001	[Organ]	
		(2) MS 1220	[Alto]	
		(3) MS 1221	[Tenor]	
		(4) MS 1222	[Tenor]	c. 1640
		(5) MS 1223	[Bass]	
		(6) MS 1224	[Bass]	
D	Barnard's *First Book of Selected Church Music*			1641
E	St George's Chapel Library, Windsor:	(1) MS 1a	[Alto]	
		(2) MS 2	[Alto]	
		(3) MS 2a	[Alto]	c. 1660
		(4) MS 3	[Tenor]	
		(5) MS 4	[Bass]	
F	St John's College, Oxford:	MS 315	[Organ]	c. 1660
G	British Library, London:	Add. MS 30478	[Tenor]	c. 1664
H	University of California, Berkeley:	MS M2 C645	[Organ]	c. 1670
I	Wimborne Minster Library:	(1) MS P11	[Alto]	
		(2) MS P14	[Tenor]	
		(3) MS P16	[Tenor]	c. 1670
		(4) MS P15	[Bass]	
J	York Minster Library: The 8 'Gostling' part-books			c. 1675
K	British Library, London:	Add. MS 17784	[Bass]	c. 1675
L	Christ Church Library, Oxford:	(1) MS 437	[Organ]	c. 1675
		(2) MS 438	[Organ]	c. 1680

continued overleaf

M   Royal College of Music, London: Printed Music 1 A 1   [Alto]   *c.* 1680
N   St Paul's Cathedral, London: (1) An un-numbered tenor part-book ⎫ *c.* 1680
                                           (2) An un-numbered bass part-book ⎬

Other sources consulted but not collated include Tudway's early 18th-century vocal score –
BM Harl. MS 7338, and three part-books in the library of Gloucester Cathedral copied from D
shortly after the Commonwealth. The text is to be found in Clifford's *Divine Services
and Anthems* . . . . of 1663.

Editorial Method:

Small notes, small accidentals, cautionary accidentals in brackets, and crossed slurs are editorial.
Since the earliest manuscript sources date from more than 40 years after the composer's death,
disparities in textual underlay are not listed in the variants. The organ part is a conflation of the
five listed sources, and only conflicting, not complementary variants are noted.

Variants:

Bar	/	Stave	/ Beat /	Source	/	Variant
2	/	4	/ 4 /	K	/	crotchet D♭
2	/	6	/ 4 /	H	/	quavers B♭, A♭ in tenor of L.H.
6	/	5	/ 1 /	L(2)	/	crotchet F in alto of R.H.
6	/	6	/ 2 /	L(2)	/	crotchet F in L.H. as in tenor voice part
6	/	2	/ 2–3 /	D, E(1) & (2), I(1) & M	/	minim F
7	/	2 & 4	/ 1 /	B, I(1) & M	/	minim
7	/	2, 3 & 4	/ 1 /	C(2)–(6)	/	minim with pause mark
8	/	2	/ 2 /	I(1)	/	crotchet D♭
10	/	4	/ 1–2 /	B	/	upper minim C
11–12	/	2	/ 2–1 /	I(1)	/	three A♭s – crotchet, minim, crotchet
11–12	/	5	/ 3–1 /	C(1)	/	dotted crotchet D♭, quaver C, crotchet A♭
12	/	2	/ 2–3 /	A & C(2)	/	two crotchet D♭s
12–13	/	4	/ 2–2 /	B	/	crotchet B♭, minim C, minim F [?]
13	/	5	/ 1–3 /	C(1)	/	dotted minim F – no rest in R.H.
15	/	3	/ 1 /	J	/	crotchet D♭ in Cantoris book [?]
17	/	2 & 5	/ 1 /	I(1) & L(2)	/	♭ to G in alto parts
17	/	2	/ 3 /	I(1)	/	crotchet F
17–18	/	5	/ 4–3 /	F	/	D♭s and Cs a third below the top of R.H.
18	/	5	/ 4 /	C(1)	/	R.H. has a top F
19	/	4	/ 2 /	B	/	low B♭ for 'our' – also in repeat
after 26	/	4	/ /	B	/	'Amen' set to low minim B♭ and upper semibreve F with a pause mark

12. HOSANNA TO THE SON OF DAVID

Edited by
ANTHONY GREENING

ORLANDO GIBBONS
(1583 — 1625)

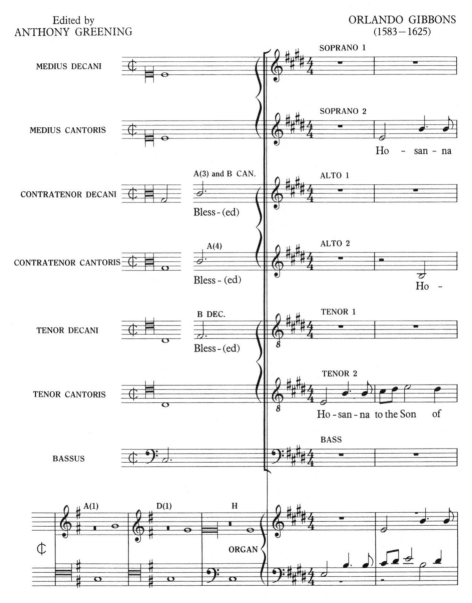

For Editorial Note see page 112.

This anthem is available separately.

*Indications in source A1:-(1) Verse, (2) Full, (3) Verse, (4) Full.

Editorial Note

Sources:

A	Durham Cathedral Library:				
	(1) MS A1	[Organ]	c. 1635	(7) MS C9	c. 1635
	(2) MS C2*			(8) MS C10	c. 1635
	(3) MS C4			(9) MS C11 [Tenor]	c. 1640
	(4) MS C5	[Alto]	c. 1635	(10) MS C15	c. 1625
	(5) MS C6				
	(6) MS C7			(11) MS C16	c. 1640
				(12) MS C17 [Bass]	c. 1675
				(13) MS C19	c. 1675

B	Barnard's *First Book of Selected Church Music*			1641
C	St John's College, Oxford:	MS 180	[Bass]	c. 1630
D	Christ Church Library, Oxford:	(1) MS 1001	[Organ]	c. 1640
		(2) MS 1012	[Bass]	c. 1670
		(3) MS 525	[Score]	c. 1675
		(4) MS 47	[Score]	c. 1680
E	York Minster Library:	(1) MS M 29 (S)	[Bass]	c. 1630
		(2) The 'Gostling' part-books		c. 1675
F	British Library, London:	(1) Add. MSS 30478 & 9	[Tenor]	c. 1664
		(2) Add. MS 17784	[Bass]	c. 1675
		(3) Royal Music Library: MS 23m3	[Bass]	c. 1695
G	St Michael's College, Tenbury:	(1) MS 1442	[Bass]	c. 1670
		(2) MS 1023	[Score]	c. 1690
H	University of California, Berkeley:	MS M2 C645	[Organ]	c. 1680
I	Gloucester Cathedral Library: an un-numbered tenor part-book,			
	probably copied from B			c. 1675
J	Fitzwilliam Museum, Cambridge:	(1) MS 88	[Scores]	c. 1677
		(2) MS 117		c. 1683
K	St Paul's Cathedral, London: one tenor and two bass part-books			
	with no shelf marks			c. 1680

Word-books:	1	Bodleian Library, Oxford: MS Rawl Poet 23	c. 1635
	2	Clifford's *The Divine Services and Anthems*	1664
	3	British Library: Harl MS 6346	c. 1670

Other later sources which have been consulted but not collated include:–

Three scores in the British Library –

Harl MS 7339, which is Tudway's score dating from about 1720;

Add. MS 31405, a full vocal score of similar date;

Add. MS 30087 – J. Bishop's 19th-century score of Barnard's part-books;

Two 18th-century scores in the library of Ely Cathedral – MSS 5 and 20;

Boyce's *Cathedral Music* of 1760;

Two organ parts in the library of Christ Church, Oxford; MSS 1230 and 1234;

Three 18th-century manuscripts in the library of St Michael's College, Tenbury – MSS 607, 805 and 1030.

Editorial Method:

All small notes and rests in the organ part are editorial additions to the three extant 17th-century books, A(1), D(1) and H. Crossed slurs are also editorial. Variants are not listed in the usual way, as the multiplicity of sources precludes mentioning all the differences in textual underlay; manifest errors on the part of scribes are also extremely numerous. The editor's main problem concerns the 'Verse' and 'Full' indications in many of the MSS: at the start of the anthem, many of the tenor sources are marked 'Vers:', but this is seldom countermanded – and the anthem is *invariably* included under the 'Full' anthems in all sources. None of the countertenor or soprano parts start with a 'Verse' indication with the sole exception of the Decani Countertenor from source E(2); at the same time, some of the bass parts collated indicate a 'Verse' section before their entry in bar 11, which is consequently marked 'Cho:'. The Durham organ part, A(1), also indicates 'Vers:' and 'Cho:' for the section, 'Peace in heav'n', beginning at bar 37, but starts 'Full'. The editor thinks that Gibbons may have intended a soloistic beginning, (perhaps *"in medio chori"*?), but cannot escape the conclusion that this is a 'Full' anthem, and that later scribes attributed various parts to solo singers where the composer had not intended it. A large choir might, perhaps, start with semi-chorus, the full choir entering at 'Blessed be he'.

None of the word-books agrees with the music MSS in the text, or its biblical ascriptions; so the editor has taken a consensus of the earliest MSS readings, and here presents the composite text without stipulating any of the Gospel texts.

13. HOSANNA TO THE SON OF DAVID

Edited by
JOHN MOREHEN

THOMAS WEELKES
(c.1575-1623)

St. Matthew 21, 9

For editorial note see page 121.

This anthem is available separately.

Editorial Note

Sources:

This edition is based on the following 'secular' sources:

A   Christ Church, Oxford, MSS. 56–60 (lacks Bass 2).
B   British Museum, Additional MSS. 17786–91 (contains all voice parts).
C   St. Michael's College, Tenbury, MSS. 807–811 (lacks Mean 2).
D   St. Michael's College, Tenbury, MS. 309 (contains Mean 2, Bass 1 and Bass 2 only).

The fact that this anthem does not survive in any liturgical source suggests very strongly that it was intended purely for secular use. This theory is supported by the unusual scoring and by the use of the Latin phrase 'Hosanna in excelsis Deo'. No positive order of primacy for the four sources can be established.

Variants:

The procedure in indicating variant readings is as follows: Bar. Voice part (reading downwards). Symbol in bar (tied note from a previous bar is treated as 0): Variant reading. (Source). Italic letters indicate note-values (*e.g. m* = minim, *c.* = dotted-crotchet).

Pref. staves. 1–6: omit mensuration symbol (A)/2.1.1: '-san*m.qnaqm*' (C)/2.3.1: '-san*m.qnaqm* (C)/2.4.4: omit ♮ (B)/3.2.2: omit ♯ (D)/4.2.2: omit ♯ (D)/4.6.1: *mm* for *m.c* (D)/5.2.1: omit ♯ (D)/5.2.5: 'of*qcc* Dac*vidc*' implied (D)/7.3.5: omit ♮ (A–C)/7.6.1: omit ♯ (D)/8.3.6: omit ♮ (A, B)/9.5.4: redundant ♮ (♭) (B, C)/11.3.3: omit ♮ (A,C)/12.3.2: omit ♮ (B)/12.4.3: 'the*c.qq* King*qq* (C)/13.6.3: 'be*c* the*c* (D)/14.6.1: E (B)/16.3.1: *c* (B)/16.4.5: 'that*q* com*c*eth*c* in*c* the*q* name*qc*' (C), 'that*q* com*c*eth*c* in*c* the*qq* name*c* of*q.sq* the*c* (B)/17.2.2: 'in*c* the*q.sq* name*c.* (D)/17.4.2: G (A, C)/18.1.1: 'the*q.sq* Lord*m*' (B)/18.3.1: 'of*qq* the*c*' (A), 'of*q* the*q* Lord*m*' (B)/18.5.2: omit ♮ (B)/19.2.3: omit ♯ (D)/19.3.1: omit ♮ (B)/19.3.5: omit ♮ (A, C)/20.2.2: omit ♯ (D)/20.5.5: omit ♮ (B)/20.5.6: G (D)/21.3.3–4: *q.sq* (A)/21.6.5: omit ♮ (B, D)/23.4.2: '-est*sq* heav*sq*ens*m*' implied (C)/24.1.6: '-est*sq* hea*sq*vens*s*' implied (C)/24.5.2: redundant ♮ (♭) (A, C, D)/25.3.2: 'the*c* high*c*est*mc*' (A, B is ambiguous)/25.6.2: 'in://:' (B)/26.4.1: 'high*c.qqq*est*c*' (A, B is ambiguous)/27.6.5: omit ♮ (B, D)/30.3.4: 'in*m.* the*c* high*m*est*c* (A)/31.5.3: '-est*c* hea*m*vens*m*' (D)/33.5.3: omit ♮ (A)/35.3.4: 'ex*qc*el*qqc*' (A), 'ex*qc*el*qsisq* De*coc*' (B)/35.4.2: '-na*m.* in*c.* ex*qc*el*c*sis*m* (*sic*) De*com*, De*mom.*, De*co*' (B)/ 35.6.1: omit ♮ (B)/36.1.3: '-cel*qsisq* De*coc*' (B)/36.2.2: omit ♯ (A, D)/36.2.2: '-cel*qqc*csis*m*' (A)/36.4.2: 'ex*c*.cel*qcm.*' (A)/37.3.1: '-cel*c*.sis*q* Dec.*qqqqqoc*' (B)/37.5.2: 'ex*qc*el*qsisq* De*coc*' (B, D)/38.3.3: omit ♮ (A)/38.3.4: '-sis*qc*' (C)/38.5.3: omit ♯ (D)/38.6.4: '-sis*q* De*cos*, De*mos*' (B)/39.3.2: '-sis*qqq* De*cos*' (B)/39.3.3: omit ♮ (B)/40.1.1: omit ♯ (B)/40.2.1: omit pause (D)/40.5.1: omit pause (D).

Editorial Method:

The organ part and the crossed slurs are editorial. Accidentals in round brackets are cautionary and not optional. Italicised text indicates that positive underlay variants are to be found in the list of variant readings.

Acknowledgements:

Grateful acknowledgement is made to the governing bodies of the libraries concerned.

14. IF YE LOVE ME

Edited by
PETER LE HURAY

THOMAS TALLIS
(c. 1505–1585)

St. John 14, 15–17

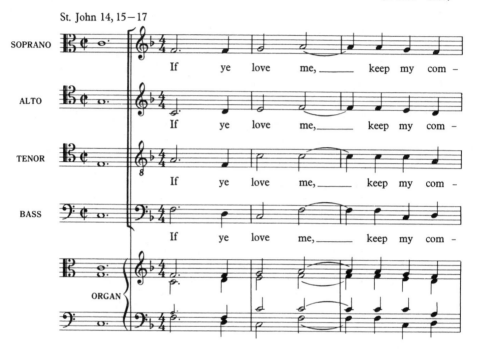

Sources:

1 John Day, *Certaine notes set forthe in foure and three partes*, 1565
2 Durham, Cathedral Library, MS A3 (0) c. 1635
3 Oxford, Bodleian Library, MSS Mus.sch.e.420-2 (Ct 1&2, B) c. 1548
Also Durham, Cathedral Library, MSS C11 (TD) c. 1660, C17 (BD) c. 1675,
C19 (B) c. 1675; London, British Museum, Add.MSS 15166 (Tr) c. 1570, 29289
(A) c. 1625, 30478-9; New York, Public Library, Drexel MSS 4180-4 (CATB)
c. 1625; Oxford, Christ Church, MS 6 (0) c. 1630.

Editorial Method:

All bar-lines, crossed slurs, and symbols printed small are editorial.

Variants:

4.i.1: *c.q* (3) / 4.ii.1: *c.q* (3) / 6.i.3-7. i.1:*m* G only (3) / 9.iv.2: *c* and *c*-rest (3).
This edition is based upon the one in *The Treasury of English Church Music*, Volume
2, by permission of Blandford Press Ltd. The anthem may be sung by two altos,
tenor and bass, in which case the music should be transposed down a tone.

This anthem is available separately (from O.U.P.)

*pronounced 'sprit'

126

15. I HEARD A VOICE

Edited by
ANTHONY GREENING
Revelation 14, 13

THOMAS TOMKINS
(1572 – 1656)

Source: *Musica Deo Sacra,* 1668

Editorial Method: Small notes, small accidentals, cautionary accidentals in brackets, and the crossed slur are editorial.

© Oxford University Press 1978

16. JUSTORUM ANIMAE

Edited by
ANTHONY GREENING

WILLIAM BYRD
(1543—1623)

Offertory for All Saints' Day
Wisdom of Solomon: 3, 1—3

Source: *Gradualia*, Book 1, 1605
Editorial Method:
The text in the source is spaced so as to leave little room for conjecture on underlay.
The keyboard reduction is editorial.

ma - nu De - - i sunt, et non tan - get il - los, et

- - nu De - - i sunt, et non tan - get il - los, et

- - nu De - - i sunt, et non tan - get il - los, et

- nu De - i sunt, De - i sunt, et non tan - get il - los

in ma - nu De - i sunt, et

non tan - get il - los tor - men - tum mor - tis,

non tan - get il - los tor - men - tum mor - tis, tor - men - tum

non tan - get il - los tor - men - tum mor - tis, tor - men - tum

tor - men - tum mor - tis, tor - men - tum mor - tis, tor - men - tum

non tan - get il - los tor - men - tum

English version
The souls of the righteous are in the hand of God, and there no torment shall touch them.
In the sight of the unwise they seemed to die: but they are in peace.

17. LAETENTUR COELI

Edited by
ROGER BRAY

WILLIAM BYRD
(1543–1623)

Sarum Respond, Advent

Sources: *Liber primus Sacrarum Cantionum* (1589), Nos. 28–29. Oxford, Christ Church, MSS 984–8 (1580s), No. 46. Tenbury, St. Michael's College, MS 389 (late 16th century), a single part-book not used in this edition.

Apart from minor variations in underlay and ligatures (not noted in this edition), the printed source and the Oxford manuscript source are the same with the following two exceptions: clef of Bass: C^5 in MS source (equivalent of F^3 of printed source) – bar 21 Soprano: MS source has no B♯ (= B♮).

This piece is an excellent example of terraced scoring, implying that it could be sung at various suitable pitches. It is quite reasonable to sing it a tone lower for the same voices, or up a semitone or a tone for two soprano voices (one high, one low), alto, tenor, and bass.

Fine

Fine

48 Secunda pars

English version
Rejoice, O heavens, and be joyful, O earth.
Give praise, O hills, for our Lord shall come
and show mercy to his humble people.
There shall rise up in those days justice and
abundance of peace.

18. LET THY MERCIFUL EARS

Edited by
W. S. COLLINS

(Formerly attributed to
THOMAS WEELKES)

Collect for the Tenth Sunday after Trinity

For Editorial Note see page 151.

This anthem is available separately.

© Oxford University Press 1969

1. G♯ A E are rests in Br. Lib. Add. MS. 30478.

Editorial Note

Fellowes's attribution of this anthem to Thomas Weelkes resulted from his use of the sources at Peterhouse College, Cambridge, where the anthem appears without ascription next to Weelkes's *Short Service for Four Voices*. All ascribed sources for the composition name Mudd (Mudds, Muds) as the composer without distinguishing among the several 17th-century composers of that surname.

Fellowes's original edition of 1924 (T.C.M. 35) contained alto and organ parts of his own composition since the Peterhouse part-books are lacking these parts. He later found the alto part at Durham, and in the 1930's revised the edition to include most of the original alto. This version has resulted in many derived editions, which have even gone so far as a recent translation into English (*O Holy Banquet*) of a Latin adaptation (*O sacrum convivium*), all attributed to Weelkes.

Editorial Method:

Small notes, cautionary accidentals in brackets, crossed slurs, and bar lines are editorial. Punctuation follows *The Book of Common Prayer* version of the collect. Spelling has been modernized with the exception of "thorough", which may be performed as a single syllable if desired. Note values have been halved and the pitch raised a tone.

Where a choice between different underlays in the manuscripts was necessary, Fellowes's version has been used. Since it was based on the Peterhouse sources, which are probably the oldest, it is assumed to be closest to Mudd's wishes. Some choirs may wish to modernize the word "prayers" into one syllable, in which cases a version similar to Fellowes's adaptation may be used:

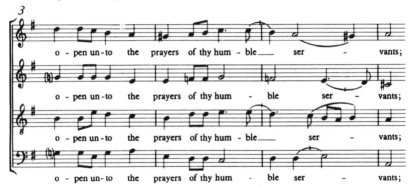

Variant readings of importance are noted in the score. Others, chiefly minor differences in text underlay, are not mentioned.

Sources:

All known 17th-century sources for the piece were used. They are: Soprano, Durham Cathedral MS C.1; Peterhouse College MS 45. Alto, Durham C.7. Tenor, Durham C. 9, C. 10, C.11, C.15; British Library Add. MSS 30478, 30479; Peterhouse 43. Bass, Durham C.16, C.17, C.19; York Minster MS M-29s; Peterhouse 36. Organ, Durham A.3.

Performance:

While unaccompanied performance would be historically permissible the composer probably would have expected some form of organ accompaniment. The present editor believes that a tempo based on slow minims will be closer to the composer's intentions than one based on crotchets.

19. LORD, FOR THY TENDER MERCY'S SAKE

Edited by
ANTHONY GREENING

FARRANT/HILTON
late 16th century

For Editorial Note see page 156.

Editorial Note

Sources:

A	Christ Church Library, Oxford:	(1) MSS 1220–1224	*c.* 1645
		(2) MS 437	*c.* 1670
B	Ely Cathedral Library:	(1) MS 4	*c.* 1670
		(2) MS 5	*c.* 1700
		(3) MS 28	*c.* 1670
C	The British Library, London:	Harl. MS 7340	1717

Text: J. Bull, *Christian Prayers and Holy Meditations* (1568)

Editorial Method:

The present edition represents a collation of the different MS sources which ascribe the music variously to 'Farrant' (A) and 'Mr John Hilton' (B & C). The final 'Amen' is found only in the latter sources. The organ part is here conflated from A(2) and B(1), and all small notes are editorial.

Variants:

Minor discrepancies of textual underlay are not noted.

Bar	/	Stave	/	Beat	/	Source	/	Variant
4	/	1 & 5	/	4	/	B(1) & (2) & C	/	two quavers, E♭ and D
4	/	4	/	4	/	C	/	lower B♭ quavers
9	/	3	/	1	/	C	/	B♭
14	/	6	/	1–4	/	A(2)	/	minims B♭ and C
14	/	2 & 4	/	3–4	/	C	/	dotted crotchet, quaver
15	/	1	/	1–2	/	C	/	dotted crotchet, quaver
16	/	1	/	2	/	C	/	E♭
18	/	3	/	1	/	B(1) & C	/	C
19	/	4	/	2	/	C	/	upper A♭
20	/	1 & 3	/	3–4	/	C	/	dotted crotchet, quaver
20	/	2	/	4	/	C	/	quavers E♭, D♭

20. MISERERE MEI

Edited by
JOHN MOREHEN

WILLIAM BYRD
(1542/3—1623)

Psalm, 51, 1

Source: Byrd's *Liber Secundus Sacrarum Cantionum*, 1591 (copy consulted Christ Church, Oxford, Mus. 489—493).

Editorial Method: Small accidentals, cautionary accidentals in brackets and the keyboard part are editorial. Ligatures indicated thus ⌐⌐.

This anthem is available separately.

1) Bar 23 (Soprano): the ♭ in the key-signature is present only at the upper pitch; the ♮ to the D is therefore not strictly editorial.

English version
Have mercy upon me, O God, after thy great goodness:
according to the multitude of thy mercies do away mine offences.

21. O CLAP YOUR HANDS

Edited by
JOHN MOREHEN

ORLANDO GIBBONS
(1583 – 1625)

from Psalm 47 (with Gloria)

For Editorial Note see page 208.

This anthem is available separately.

6

9

18

21

27

30

33

36

39

42

48

57

60

63

69

72

87

96

99

102

105

108

111

121

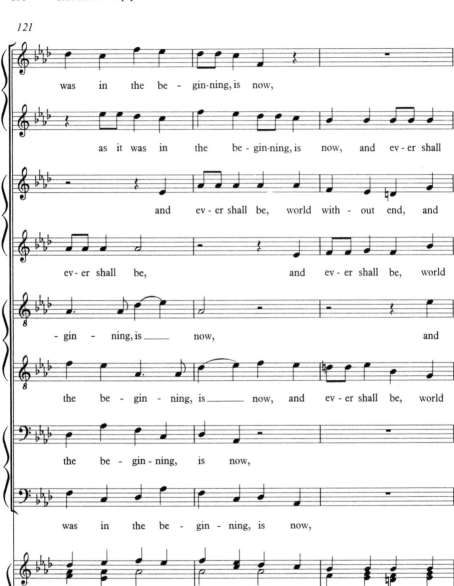

124

127

130

with-out end. A - men, world with - out end. A - men.

with-out end,_____world with-out end. A - men.

world with-out end. A - men, with - out end. A - men.

world with - out end, world with - out end. A - men.

with - out end. A - men, with - out end. A - men.

with - out end, world with-out end. A - men, A - men.

world with - out end. A - men.

with - out end, with - out end. A - men.

Editorial Note

This work was performed, probably for the first time, on the 17th May, 1622, when Gibbons and his friend William Heyther were admitted to the degree of Doctor of Music at Oxford.

Sources:

A. York Minster Library, the 'Gostling' part-books. This is a complete set of manuscripts dating from about 1675. The pagination is as follows: Medius Decani (p. 144); Medius Cantoris (p. 104); Contratenor Decani (p. 139); Contratenor Cantoris (p. 146); Tenor Decani (p. 108); Tenor Cantoris (p. 102); Bassus Decani (p. 143); Bassus Cantoris (p. 128).

B. British Library, Additional MS. 29289, f.95v. This Contratenor part-book appears to date from about 1630; it may well have been used in St. Paul's Cathedral.

Editorial Method:

Editorial and 'cancelling' accidentals are printed in small size; cautionary accidentals are printed in brackets *when they are not present in the sources*. Redundant accidentals are omitted. The spelling and punctuation have been modernized. The keyboard reduction is editorial.

Variants:

Variants are set out in the following order: bar. stave. symbol in bar (tied note from previous bar treated as O): variant. Note-values are shown in italics (e.g. *c*=crotchet, *sq·*=dotted-semi-quaver). All variants refer to the York MSS. unless otherwise stated. Prefatory staves.4: omit mensuration symbol / 6.8.3: E♭ / 6.4.5: the 2 E♮s are slurred / 9.4.4: omit ♭ / 10.5.2–3: omit accidentals / 16.2.1: redundant ♭ / 17.2.4: 'and to ·//·' but the underlay is correct from the 2nd note of bar 18 / 19.4.2: possibly up$^{c·q}$on^{c} (29289) / 21.6.1: redundant ♭ / 22.4.2: the^{q} great^{c} King^{c} up^{c}on$^{c·q}$ / 32.6.1: C / 32.7.2: omit ♭ / 38.4.3: he$^{c·}$ri^{qqq}c$^{}$tage$^{c·}$ for^{q} (29289) / 44.4.3: the^{q} wor^{c}chip^{q} of^{q} Ja^{c}cob^{c} whom^{c} he^{c} lov^{q}ed^{q} (29289) / 45.6.1: D♭ / 47.4.2: whom^{qq} he$^{q m·}$ lov^{c}ed^{m} / 48.4.3: no pause / 56.4.2: and^{c} the^{m} Lord^{m} with$^{c·}$ the^{q} sound^{c} of^{q} the^{q} trum$^{m·}$pet^{c} the^{q} sound^{q} / 59.4.1: omit ♭ / 59.4.2–3: omit both accidentals (both sources) / 60.4.5: omit ♭ / 61.4.3: and^{qq} (*sic*) the^{q} Lord^{m} with$^{c·}$ the^{q} sound^{c} of^{m} the^{mc} trum^{c}pet^{c} (A♭, A♭, A♭, D♭, E♭, C, F, B♭, A♭, G, A♭, A♭) / 68.4.3: un^{qc}to^{c} our^{c} God^{c} / 75.4.2: our^{c} King^{q} / 78.4.3: is^{q} the^{q} / 79.4.3: all^{c} the^{c} earth^{m} sing^{m} / 83.4.2: E♭ / 87.4.4: the^{m} hea^{c}then^{m} / 90.6.3: B♭ / 96.4.4: his^{c} ho^{cc}ly^{m} seat^{c} / 104.8.6: redundant ♮ / 110.4.4: to^{q} the^{q} Fa^{c}(G)ther^{c}(F) and^{c} to^{c} the^{c} Son^{m} the^{c} Son^{m} (29289) / 120.4.1–2: and^{c} is^{c} (29289); presumably the other books of this set gave 'and^{c} is^{c}' at bars 121 (Tenor 1) and 122 (Tenor 2) / 123.6.2: no accidental / 124.4.1: with^{c}out^{c} end^{c} A^{c}men^{c} (29289) / 125.7.4: no accidental / 126.8.4: no accidental / 128.5.4: F in addition / 131.5.3: 'world ·//·' / 133.3,6,7: m

Grateful acknowledgement is made to the governing bodies of the libraries concerned.

22. O LORD, ARISE

Edited by
ROGER BRAY

THOMAS WEELKES
(c. 1575 – 1623)

Psalm 132, 8 – 9
Te Deum, 22

Sources:

London, British Library, MSS Add. 17786–91 (early C17th); S1, S2, A1, T, B1, B2.
London, British Library, MSS Add. 17792–6 (early C17th); S1, A1, A2, T, B2.
London, Royal College of Music, MSS 1045–51 (early C17th); S1, S2, A1, A2, T, B2.
New York, Public Library, MSS Drexel 4180–5 (c. 1620); all voices.
Tenbury, St. Michael's College, MS 1382 (1617); T.

Editorial Method:

This is a performing edition. A full list of variants, especially of underlay which differs extensively between sources, would take up too much space, and in any case such a critical edition is available elsewhere (*Musica Britannica*, Vol. 23). All accidentals in ordinary print are present in at least one source, or are consequent or retrospective. Editorial accidentals are printed small.

21

25

37

40

23. O LORD, IN THY WRATH

Edited by
JOHN MOREHEN

ORLANDO GIBBONS
(1583–1625)

Psalm 6, 1–4

For Editorial Note see page 239.

This anthem is available separately.

*This F may be a scribal error for E♭.

Editorial Note

The only source of this fine anthem is a set of seven part-books known as the 'Barnard' manuscripts (Royal College of Music, MSS. 1045-1051); the Decani Bass part-book is missing. The manuscripts are thought to have been compiled *c.* 1625-*c.* 1635 by John Barnard, a Minor Canon of St. Paul's Cathedral. They appear to have served as printer's copy for some of the items later printed in Barnard's *First Book of Selected Church Musick*, the first edition of which may have been published in 1641. The Barnard manuscripts provide what appears to be an unusually accurate text; the only errors are that some part-books give *hear* for *heal* in bar 27.

Two of the four six-part anthems in Barnard's publication are by Gibbons, and the editor could be excused for not wanting to include a further one. It is surprising, however, that Barnard should have passed over 'O Lord, in thy wrath' in favour of the inferior 'Lift up your heads'.

No organ score of this anthem has survived, and the keyboard part printed in this edition is editorial. The extent to which the organ was used during services in the early seventeenth century no doubt varied a great deal, though it appears from the Chapter records of several Cathedrals that it was customary for the organist to take his place in the choir whenever it was not absolutely essential for him to be in the organ loft. The keyboard part may therefore be regarded as wholly optional. Accidentals in round brackets are cautionary and not optional.

24. O LORD, THE MAKER

Edited by
PETER LE HURAY

WILLIAM MUNDY
(c. 1530–1591)

The King's Primer 1545

For Editorial Note see page 247.

This anthem is available separately (from OUP).

© 1965 by Blandford Press Ltd.

Editorial Note

Sources:

1   John Barnard, *The First Book of Selected Church Musick,* 1641
2   Durham Cathedral Library, MS. A3 (O), *c.* 1635
3   London, British Library, Add. MS. 29289 (A), *c.* 1625
4   New York Public Library, Drexel MSS. 4180–3 (C, A, T, B,), *c.* 1625
5   Christ Church, Oxford, MSS. 1220, 1222–4 (AD, TC, BD, BC), *c.* 1640

Also New York Public Library, Drexel MS. 5469 (O), *c.* 1630; Christ Church, Oxford, MS. 6 (O), *c.* 1630, MS. 88 (O), *c.* 1660, and MS. 1001 (O), *c.* 1640.

Editorial Method:
Bar-lines, small notes, small accidentals, cautionary accidentals in round brackets, and crossed slurs are editorial.   Accidentals in square brackets are found in some, but not all, sources.

Variants: 4.ii.3: ♭ (4)/2.r.h.1–2: A♭ (2)/5.ii.4: A♮ (4)/6.ii.2–7.ii.1: *cm* (4)/7.i.1: *cc* (4)/
7.i.2: ♭ (4)/7.ii.2: *c.q*B♭ (4)/9.ii.3: through *q* thy *q* (4)/10.ii.3: ♭ (3) (4), and also 11.ii.3/
14.ii.1: ♭ (4)/16.i.3: C (1)/ 16–24: the antiphonal arrangement of dec. and can. is unique to 1/19: with dream nor fantasy (4)/22.i.3: *m* (1)/23.ii.1–2: *c.q* (4)/29.i.3: *m.*
(no *c*-rest) (4)/33.ii.1–34.ii.1: *cccm* (4)/38.ii.1: ♭ (4)/42.i.2–end: missing in (4); this fifth part is not essential to the harmony, and may well be a seventeenth-century addition. There are no repeat marks in (3), or (4); the repeat is fully written out in (2), with minor (unrecorded) variations./45.iii.1–46.iii.2: *mmc.*D*q*E♭ (4)/46.v.2: ♭ (4).

The organ part differs from the voice parts in a few small details, notably in bars 7, 31-2 and 42. The alternative reading suggested by the organ part for the soprano, bars 31-2, may be preferred: our*q* pe*q*tim(C)tic(B)on*m*(A).

This edition has been reprinted from *The Treasury of English Church Music,* Volume 2, be permission of Blandford Press Ltd.

25. O NATA LUX

Edited by
ANTHONY GREENING

THOMAS TALLIS
(c. 1505 – 1585)

O.H. for Lauds on the Feast of the Transfiguration

Source: 'Cantiones quae ab argumento sacrae vocantur' 1575.

Editorial Method: Small accidentals and the keyboard reduction are editorial.

This anthem is available separately.

English version
O Light of light, by love inclined,
Jesu, redeemer of mankind,
With loving-kindness deign to hear
From suppliant voices praise and prayer

Thou who to raise our souls from hell
Didst deign in fleshly form to dwell,
Vouchsafe us, when our race is run,
In thy fair Body to be one.

26. O PRAISE THE LORD

Edited by
ANTHONY GREENING

ADRIAN BATTEN
(1591–1637?)

Psalm 117

For Editorial Note see page 255. This anthem is available separately.

Editorial Note

Sources:

A	Barnard's *First Book of Selected Church Music*			1641
B	Durham Cathedral Library:	(1) MS A6	[Organ]	*c.* 1640
		(2) MS C11 ⎫		*c.* 1640
		(3) MS C12 ⎬ [Tenor]		*c.* 1675
		(4) MS C15 ⎭		*c.* 1625
		(5) MS C17 ⎱ [Bass]		*c.* 1675
		(6) MS C19 ⎰		*c.* 1675
C	British Library, London:	(1) Add. MSS 30478 & 9	[Tenor]	1664
		(2) Add. MS 17784	[Bass]	*c.* 1675
D	Gloucester Cathedral Library:	2 tenor and 1 bass un-numbered part-books, probably copied from A		*c.* 1665
E	University of California, Berkeley:	MS M2 C645	[Organ]	*c.* 1680
F	Christ Church Library, Oxford:	(1) MSS 1220 - 1224 — Alto, tenor & bass parts		*c.* 1680
		(2) & (3) MSS 437 & 438	[Organ]	*c.* 1680
G	St John's College, Oxford:	MS 315	[Organ]	*c.* 1660
H	Wimborne Minster Library:	1 tenor and 1 bass part		*c.* 1670
I	York Minster Library:	the 4 Decani books of the 'Gostling' part-books – MSS M 1/5-8 (S)		*c.* 1675

Other sources which have been consulted, but not collated, include a later bass book in the British Library, (Royal Mus. Lib. 23 m 3), an 18th-century bass part in the Bodleian Library, Oxford, (MS Mus. d 162), and scores in both the Fitzwilliam Library, Cambridge, (MS 116), and the British Library, (Add. MS 30087).

Editorial Method:

Small notes, cautionary accidentals in brackets, and crossed slurs are editorial. The alternative accompaniments given for the last two bars clearly represent two versions of lost originals.

Variants:

Bar	/	Stave	/	Beat	/	Source	/	Variant
5	/	5	/	4	/	F(2) & G	/	quaver rest followed by quaver E♭
5	/	3	/	3	/	H	/	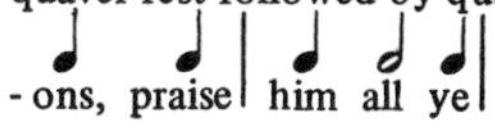 - ons, praise him all ye
10	/	2	/	1-3	/	F(1)	/	crotchet, minim
11	/	2	/	2-3	/	I(1) & F	/	minim A♭
13	/	3	/	3-4	/	B(4), F & H	/	dotted crotchet & quaver underlaid for ' - ful - '
13	/	4	/	1-2	/	B(6)	/	two crotchets underlaid for ' - ful - '
13-14	/	4	/	3-2	/	Bass	/	' - ness' on 4-beat note; subsequent crotchet lacking
19	/	1	/	4	/	I(1)	/	♮ to D
24	/	3	/	2	/	H	/	crotchet A♮

The ligature in bar 22 is from B(5) & (6) and F

27. O QUAM GLORIOSUM

Edited by
ROGER BRAY

WILLIAM BYRD
(1542/3 – 1623)

For editorial note see page 272.

This anthem is available separately.

© Oxford University Press 1976

BENEDICTIO ET CLARITAS
SECUNDA PARS

Editorial Note

CS   *Liber Primus Sacrarum Cantionum* (1589), Nos. 22-3.

Ch   Oxford, Christ Church, MSS 979-83 (Baldwin's Partbooks, 1570s and 1580s), No. 9 (lacking Tenor).

Dow   Oxford, Christ Church, MSS 984-8 (Robert Dow's Partbooks, 1580s), No. 30.

Bal·   London, British Library, R.M. 24 d 2 (Baldwin's Commonplace Book, this piece copied in the 1590s?), No. 66. In score.

The work appears also in other incomplete sources which have not been collated, either because of the fact that they were in all likelihood copied after the appearance of the printed version (and not through any automatic mistrust of their lateness), or because of their incompleteness. These sources include Chelmsford, Essex Record Society, MS D/p 1 (Bass); Tenbury, St Michael's College, MSS 341-4 (lacking Bass), 389, 1486; Worcester, Spetchley Park, 'Willmott' MS.

This piece may well have been copied into *Ch* and *Dow* before 1589. It is not at present possible to say whether the version in *Bal* (probably copied after the appearance of the printed version) was copied from *Ch* (another Baldwin MS) or *CS* or neither. In *Bal* the Alto part gets out of step between bars 43 and 70, as does the Tenor in bar 100, in each case the part in question having 10 beats in a bar against all the other voices' 8 beats (two-bars worth in this edition) in Baldwin's scored and barred version. *Bal* also exchanges the two Soprano parts in the *Secunda Pars* (an odd thing if one is copying from a printed partbook set).

In the commentary following, entries are given in the following order: bar number, name of part, source (as above), variant. Differences in underlay are not noted, since even in *CS* many phrases are marked merely with a 'ditto' sign, and common sense was apparently required then as now.

Clef B C⁵ in *Dow* / 6 S² *Ch* B♮ / 7 S² *Ch* no ♮ for ¹C; no ♭ for ²B in any source, though B♭ signified by fact that accidentals apply only to note immediately following / 13 S² *Ch* no B♮ / 21-2 S¹ *Dow* breve for first semibreve / 51 A no ♭ for ²B in any source / 56 S² *Ch* no B♮ / 59 A no B♭ in any source / 64 B *Dow* no B♮ / 65 T no ♭ for ²B in any source / 71 S² *CS* time sig omitted at beginning appears here / 72 S² *Dow* B♮ / 75 T *Dow* B♭ / 81 S¹ *Ch* E♮; / T *Dow* no B♮ / 86 S¹ no ♮ for ²C in any source / 90 S¹ *CS, Ch, Bal* no ♮ for ²F though *CS* starts new line with this note / 99 T *Dow* F♯ / 108 S¹ *Bal* no B♮ / 120 B *Bal* no E♭.

Transposition down a tone is implied by the clefs, though by this time it was not as automatically applied as it had been earlier in the century. Small accidentals, and the keyboard reduction are editorial.

English Version

O how glorious is the kingdom wherein all the saints rejoice in Christ; clothed in white robes they follow the Lamb whithersoever he goeth, praising God and saying: Blessing, and glory, and wisdom, and thanksgiving, and honour, and power, and might, be unto our God for ever and ever.   Amen.

28. SALVATOR MUNDI
(WITH ALL OUR HEARTS)

Edited by
PETER LE HURAY

THOMAS TALLIS
(c. 1505 – 1585)

Sources: Tallis and Byrd, *Cantiones, quae ab argumento sacrae vocantur*, 1575 (Latin version); John Barnard, *The First Book of Selected Church Musick*, 1641 (English version); and University of California, MS. M2. C645 late 17th century (organ reduction, English version only).
The musical texts of the Latin and English versions are by no means identical, as may be seen from this conflation.

Editorial Method: Bar-lines, small notes in the organ part, names of parts, small accidentals, the crossed tie, and cautionary accidentals in brackets are editorial. Where the music of the English and Latin versions differs, notes to be used with the English text are printed small, with upward stems.

This edition has been reprinted from *The Treasury of English Church Music* volume 2 by permission of Blandford Press Ltd.

This anthem is available separately (from OUP).

English version of Latin text
O Saviour of the world, who by thy cross and precious blood hast redeemed us.
Save us, and help us, we humbly beseech thee, O Lord. Amen.

29. SING JOYFULLY

Edited by
JOHN MOREHEN

WILLIAM BYRD
(1542/3 – 1623)

Psalm 81, 1 – 4

Sources: This anthem, one of the most popular of its period, survives in about a hundred printed or manuscript sources of the early 17th century (no 16th-century sources are extant). No overall stemmatic relationship of sources can be established, and this edition mainly represents the results of a collation of the earliest sources with those later sources which are of proven authority for music by Chapel Royal composers. The organ part is from Durham Cathedral Ms. A1, p. 167. The full sources for this piece are listed in Daniel and Le Huray *The Sources of English Church Music* (1967).

Editorial Method: Small notes, small rests, and small accidentals are editorial.

30. TEACH ME, O LORD

Edited by
JOHN MOREHEN

WILLIAM BYRD
(1542/3 – 1623)

Psalm 119, 33–38; Gloria

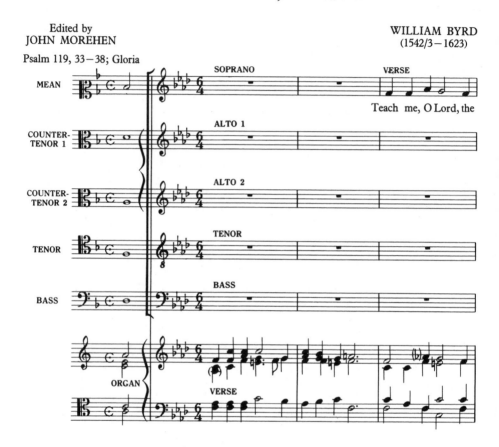

Teach me, O Lord, the

Sources: This Festal Psalm exists in two versions. That printed here (the only one for which an organ part exists) is in the following sources: John Barnard's *First Book of Selected Church Musick*, 1641 (**A**); New York Public Library, the 'Chirk Castle' partbooks, *c.* 1625, lacking Mean (**B**); Christ Church, Oxford, Ms. 6, the organ-book to source **B**, *c.* 1625 (**C**); Lambeth Palace Library, Ms. 764, Bass, *c.* 1635 (**D**); York Minster Library, the 'Dunnington-Jefferson' Ms., M–29 (S), Bass, *c.* 1640 (**E**). The alternative version is printed in *Tudor Church Music*, II, p. 30.
Most sources use a mensuration symbol of ₵ for the verses and ₵ for the choruses. However, **E**, which has only the full sections, has ₵ for the whole piece, and **C** uses ₵/3 for all verses other than the first.

Editorial Method: Small notes, small rests, and small accidentals are editorial. The signs ⌐ ⌐ and ⌐⌐ indicate coloration and ligatures, respectively, in at least one source. Some pause marks at the end of verses have been suppressed, and the final notes of sections have been standardized so as to complete a measure. In this edition only selected variants are shown.

way of thy sta-tutes: and I shall keep it

un-to the end.   CHORUS   Give me un-der-stand-ing, and I___

Give me un-der-stand-ing, and I___

Give me un-der-stand-ing, and I___

Give me un-der-stand-ing, and I___

Give me un-der-stand-ing, and I___

CHORUS

*D ♮ in C.

in the path of thy com-mand-e-ments: for

there-in is my de - sire. In-cline my heart un-to

In - cline my heart un - to

In - cline my heart un - to

In - cline my heart un - to

In - cline my heart un - to

CHORUS

CHORUS

★Eb in C

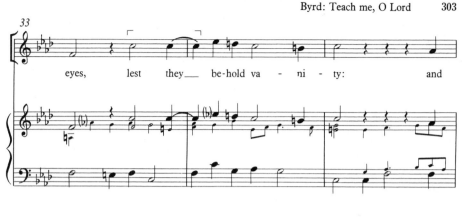

*D♮ in A.

Glo - ry be to the Fa - ther, and to ___ the Son:

and to the Ho - - - ly ___ Ghost;   As   it was   in the be - gin-

As   it was   in the be - gin-

As   it was   in the be - gin-

As   it was   in the be - gin-

As   it was   in the be - gin-

*In sources **B** and **C** this chord is an extra crotchet long, with the Countertenor 2 B♭ being preceded by a
crotchet B♭. The chorus section is preceded by a crotchet rest.

31. THIS DAY CHRIST WAS BORN
'A Carroll for Christmas day'

Edited by
JOHN MOREHEN

WILLIAM BYRD
(1542/3 – 1623)

Source: William Byrd's *Psalmes, Songs, and Sonnetts*, 1611 (Christ Church, Oxford, Printed Music 489–494). The text is an English translation of the Magnificat Antiphon at Second Vespers of Christmas Day.

Editorial Method: The proportional sign for the sections in triple metre is '3' in conjunction with coloration (indicated ⌐ ⌐), although some dotted-minim units (as reduced) in these sections are notated under the original mensuration of **C** with the appropriate adjustments to the values. Small accidentals and the keyboard reduction are editorial.

*Quaver (as reduced) in the source

★See footnote page 312

*E in the source

32. THIS IS THE RECORD OF JOHN

Edited by
PETER LE HURAY

ORLANDO GIBBONS
(1583—1625)

St. John 1:19

The accompaniment may be played by organ or viols.

For Editorial Note see page 331. Also available, ed. Fellowes, a tone higher for tenor solo and SATB (TCM42).

re - cord of John,   when the Jews   sent priests   and   Le - vites___

___ from Je - ru - sa - lem, from Je - ru - sa - lem   to   ask

*For performances with viols only G naturals may be preferred.

thou E - lias? And he said, I am not. Art__

__ thou the pro-phet? Art __ thou the pro-phet? And__ he an - swered,

sent   us.   What sayest thou of thy-self?   And

he said,   I am___ the voice of him   that cri-eth   in the wild-

87

Editorial Note

Sources: (a) Vocal parts

1. Durham Cathedral, c. 1635–8, partly in the hand of Toby Brooking, a member of the cathedral choir.

2. Cambridge, Peterhouse, c. 1637–40, partly in the hand of Thomas Wilson, organist of the college, and until 1635 a chorister at Durham.

3. Oxford, St. John's College, c. 1633–36, in the hand of John Stevens, official copyist to the Chapel Royal, and Clerk of the Cheque to the Chapel.

4. York Minster, c. 1640, linked, as are the Peterhouse books, to the Durham MSS.

Also post-Restoration sources at Lichfield and Manchester (Henry Watson Library).

(b) Organ parts

5. Durham, MS A5, c. 1638, in the hand of Henry Palmer, a member of the Durham choir,

6. Peterhouse, MS 46, c. 1638? in the hand of Thomas Wilson (see above).

Also St. Michael's College, Tenbury, MS 791, in the hand of Adrian Batten: an inferior text containing obvious errors.

(c) Scores

7. Oxford, Christ Church, MS 21, post-Restoration, possibly as late as 1734.

8. Royal College of Music, London, MS 1060: an 18th c. copy by William Hayes of a post-Restoration(?) score by Goodson.

Full source details are in   1) R. T. Daniels and P. G. le Huray: 'The Sources of English Church Music, 1544–1660', *Early English Church Music,* suppl. vol. I (St. & Bell, 1972).

and

2) John Morehen: 'The Sources of English Cathedral Music', *Dissertation for Ph.D.,* (unpublished), Cambridge, 1969.

Editorial Method:

Small notes, small rests, and small accidentals are editorial.

Variants:

There are remarkably few variants of any significance in the extant sources. 7 is the only text for the viol parts, apart from the later 8, which may well have been based upon it. 7 has therefore been used as the prime text for the present edition. Although its provenance is uncertain, it is a careful score in every respect. In view of the variants between the extant viol and organ parts, simultaneous use of viols and organ seems unlikely. Organ parts 5 and 6 are practically identical, and need almost no editorial filling-out. The solo alto part is given throughout in the organ accompaniment: there are good reasons for believing that the organist would not have doubled the voice, nonetheless, not least being the fact that certain bars are unplayable without pedals: c.f. 4, 66 and 69. The solo part is transposed in f.A2 of Peterhouse MS 44 for treble – a normal version is also to be found in this book on f.F6.

Substantial variants:

17 iii 1–9: I q am sq sq sq sq sq sq q not q (2) / 32–3: Elias is variously set as c q q, c c c, and c s – the intention seems to have been that Elias should almost be treated as a 2-syllable word / 41 iii 3:   him c, what c art c thou q, what q art c thou c (2) / 53 iv 1: pro c phet q and q he q q c (1) / 79 iv 3: that c cri q eth q in c. the q wild c. er q c m ness m (1) / 87 v 1– : Lord c, make c straight c the c way c of c the c q q Lord c (1) / 88 iv 1– : way c of c the c q q q q Lord m, the c way c of q the q (1).

'To Mr. Thomas Myriell'

33. WHEN DAVID HEARD

Edited by
JOHN MOREHEN

THOMAS TOMKINS
(1572–1656)

2 Samuel 18, 33

Sources: Thomas Tomkins *Songs of 3. 4. 5. and 6. Parts*, c. 1622 (**A**); British Library, Add. Mss. 29372-6, c. 1616 (**B**); New York Public Library, Drexel Mss. 4180-4, c. 1625 (**C**); Thomas Tomkins *Musica Deo Sacra*, 1668 (**D**). Although **A** must be accorded source primacy, due weight has been given to **B**, which not only predates **A** but which is also very closely associated with the dedicatee of this composition. Source **C**, an otherwise valuable source, appears to derive from **A** and is thus of little independent value for this piece. Source **D** has been consulted, but in view of its late date and frequently suspect text its readings have usually been disregarded where they are uncorroborated by **A** or **B**. Source **D**, however, provides the only keyboard part.

Editorial Method: Some redundant rests have been suppressed, so have some notes where they are duplicated between the hands. No attempt has been made to reconcile compatible variants between the voice and organ parts. Small notes are editorial, either new or in place of censored notes. A ligature in at least one source is indicated thus ⌐‾‾⌐. Cautionary accidentals, in round brackets, are not necessarily editorial. An accidental with a dot above (e.g. ♭) is required through modernization of the key-signature; small accidentals are editorial. In this edition only selected variants are shown.

*D provides a different version of the Countertenor 2 part, involving consecutive octaves with the organ bass.

*The spacing of the right-hand part of this bar is defective in the source.

34. WHEN DAVID HEARD

Edited by
ANTHONY GREENING

2 Samuel 18, 33

THOMAS WEELKES
(d. 1623)

For Editorial Note see page 351.

Editorial Note

Sources:

A   The British Library, London: Add. MSS 29372-7   1616
     A set of part-books copied by Thomas Myriell with an
     engraved title page bearing the heading *TRISTITIAE
     Remedium*

B   Christ Church Library, Oxford: MSS 56-60   *c.* 1620
     A set of books lacking the Bass part

C   St Michael's College Library, Tenbury: MSS 807-811   *c.* 1615
     A set of part-books wanting the 1st soprano part

(The anthem also appears in a 17th-century vocal score in the New
York Public Library – Drexel MS 4302)

Editorial Method:

Although there is no reason to suppose that Weelkes intended his
sacred choral music to be sung unaccompanied, no organ score is extant. The
keyboard reduction is therefore editorial, as are all crossed slurs showing
where the MS source(s) indicate verbal underlay. Square brackets are used
to indicate ligatures in the MS sources.

Variants:

Minor discrepancies of textual underlay are not noted.

Bar	/ Stave /	Beat	/ Source /	Variant
7	/ 4 /	1 & 2	/ C	/ minim tied from previous bar
8	/ 4 /	1	/ C	/ two quavers
18-19	/ 5 /	1-4 1-4	/ C	/ two semibreves for 'the gate'
27-28 onwards	/ 3 & 4 /	–	/ C	/ parts cross over in MS books
54	/ 1 /	1-4	/ B	/ semibreve for 'O'